My World of Science

CONDUCTORS AND INSULATORS

Angela Royston

Heinemann Library
Chicago, Illinois

Designed by Jo Hinton-Malivoire and Tinstar Design Limited
Originated by Blenheim Colour, Ltd.
Printed and bound in China by South China Printing Company
Photo research by Maria Joannou and Sally Smith

07 06 05 04 03
10 9 8 7 6 5 4 3 2 1

Library of Congress Cataloging-in-Publication Data

Royston, Angela.
  Conductors and insulators / Angela Royston.
    v. cm. – (My world of science.)
Includes bibliographical references and index.
Contents: What is a conductor? – What is an insulator? – What is electricity? – Conducting electricity – A simple circuit – Water also conducts electricity – Comparing metals – Conducting heat – Good insulators – Insulating air – Clothes – Other insulators – Using conductors and insulators together.
  ISBN 1-40340-851-3 (HC), 1-40343-164-7 (Pbk)
  1. Electric conductors–Juvenile literature. 2. Electric insulators and insulation–Juvenile literature. [1. Electricity. 2. Heat.] I. Title.
  TK3301 .R69 2003
  621.319'3–dc21
                                    2002009427
Acknowledgments
The author and publishers are grateful to the following for permission to reproduce copyright material:
pp. 4, 28 Network Photographers; pp. 5, 8, 9, 10, 12, 13, 14, 16, 18, 19, 20, 21, 22, 23 Trevor Clifford; pp. 6, 29 PhotoDisc; p. 7 Peter Gould; p. 11 G. Hopkinson/Trip; p. 15 Corbis (RF); p. 17 Getty Images; p. 24 Science Photo Library/Custom Medical Stock; p. 25 N. Price/Trip; p. 26 H. Rogers/Trip; p. 27 Tudor Photography.

Cover photograph reproduced with permission of PhotoDisc.

Every effort has been made to contact copyright holders of any material reproduced in this book. Any omissions will be rectified in subsequent printings if notice is given to the publisher.

Some words are shown in bold, **like this.** You can find out what they mean by looking in the glossary.

Contents

What Is a Conductor? 4

What Is an Insulator? 6

What Is Electricity? 8

Conducting Electricity 10

A Simple Circuit 12

Water and Electricity 14

Comparing Metals 16

Conducting Heat 18

Good Insulators 20

Insulating Air 22

Clothes 24

Other Insulators 26

Using Conductors and
    Insulators together 28

Glossary 30

More Books to Read 31

Index 32

What Is a Conductor?

A conductor lets heat or electricity pass through it. The heat from the tea passes through the metal spoon.

An electric wire conducts electricity.
Electricity passes from the plug
in the wall to the **motor** in
the hair dryer.

What Is an Insulator?

An insulator does not let heat or electricity pass through it. The handle of this wooden spoon does not get hot. Wood is an insulator.

Plastic is also a good insulator. Each of these wires is covered with plastic. Electricity from the wires cannot pass through the plastic.

What Is Electricity?

Electricity is used to make things happen. Electricity makes the toaster hot. When the toast is ready, it pops up.

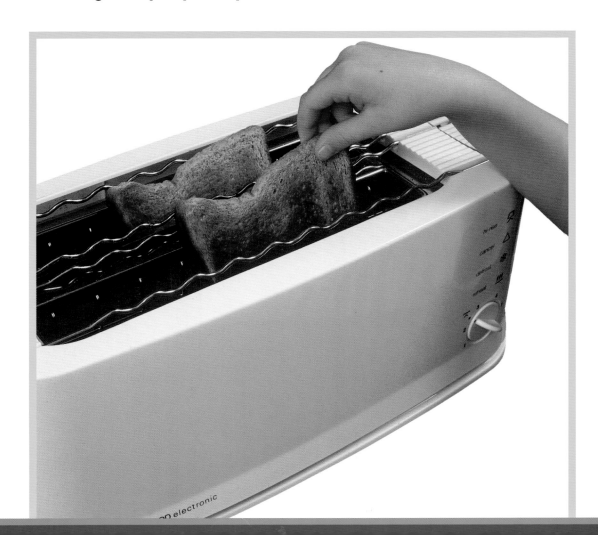

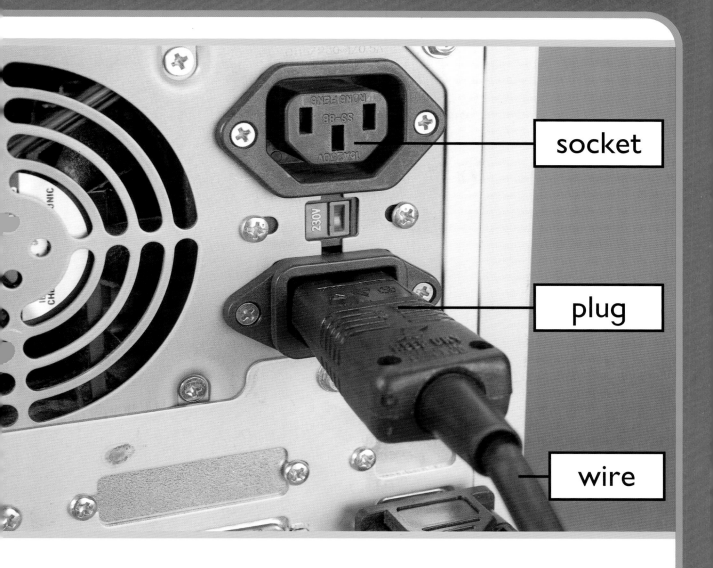

socket

plug

wire

Be safe! Do not touch bare electrical wires or electrical machines that may be hot. Never poke anything into an electric **socket** or electrical machine.

Conducting Electricity

An electrical wire is made of thin pieces of metal. The wire lets electricity pass from the plug in the wall into the television. Then it goes then back to the plug.

This train has an **engine** that runs on electricity. The electricity is conducted into the engine from the wire above the train.

A Simple Circuit

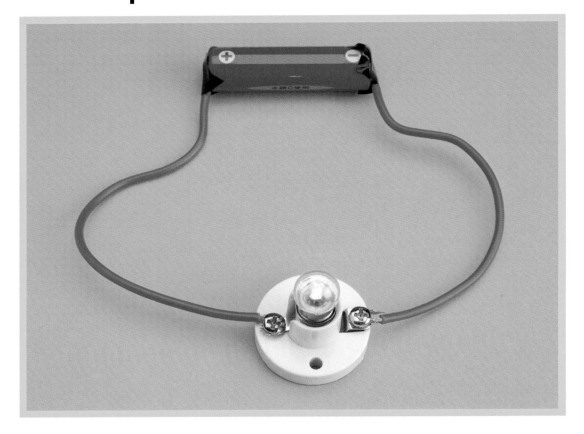

This is a simple **circuit.** The battery makes electricity. Wires conduct electricity from the battery to the light bulb and back to the battery. The electricity lights up the light bulb.

Electricity will not flow if there is a gap in the circuit. There is a gap between the wire and the battery. Electricity will not flow in this circuit.

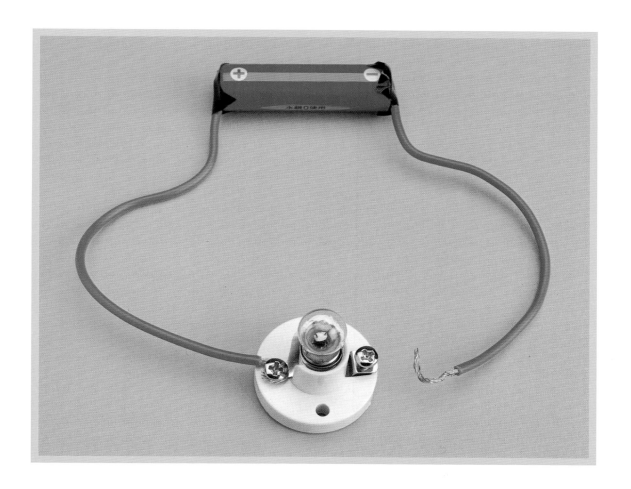

Water and Electricity

Do not touch an electrical machine or switch with wet hands. Water can conduct electricity into your body and give you an **electric shock!**

Never put electrical machines in water. This swimming pool has lights under the water, but they are safe. They have been **sealed** so that the water cannot reach them.

Comparing Metals

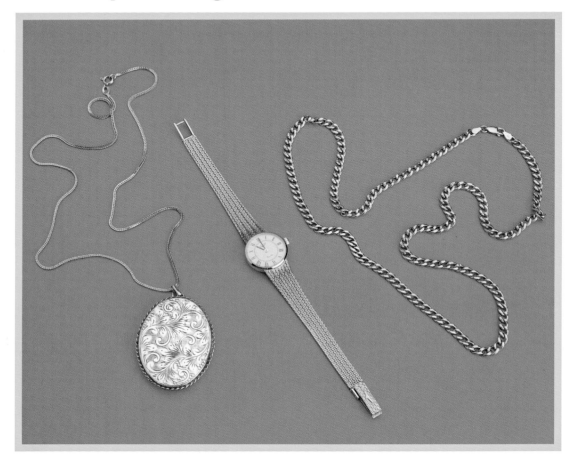

Some metals conduct electricity better than other metals. **Gold** is a good conductor of electricity.

Electric wires and cables are usually made of **copper**. Copper is another good conductor of electricity.

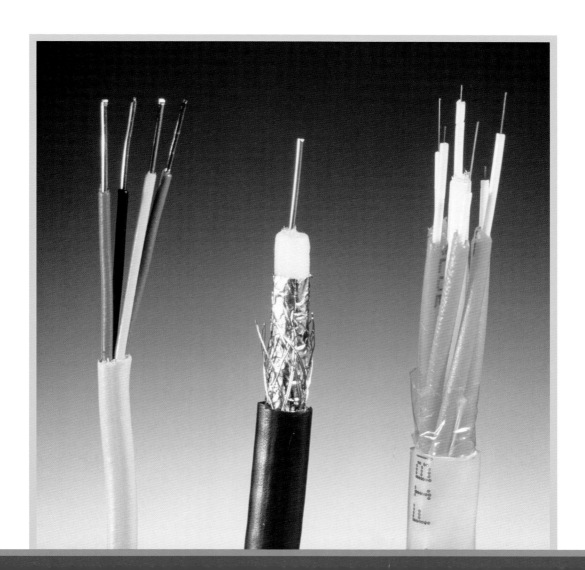

Conducting Heat

Most metals conduct heat well. When you touch metal things in summer, the metal feels warm.

This pan has **copper** on the bottom. Copper is a good heat conductor. It spreads heat across the bottom of the pan.

Good Insulators

You can test different materials to see whether they are good insulators. When this boy puts an insulator into the **circuit,** the bulb does not light.

Rubber, cloth, plastic, and wood are good insulators. A leaf is a good insulator, too. It does not let heat pass through.

Insulating Air

Air can be a good insulator. Electricity cannot pass through the air from the battery to the flashlight.

A insulated bottle has one **container** inside another. There is a space with air between them. The air stops the heat from escaping.

Clothes

Clothes are good insulators.
This blanket keeps the woman
warm. They keep warm air near
her body.

The **fleecy** linings of these coats also trap warm air. The children's hats trap air too. The mittens keep their hands warm.

Other Insulators

Wool, cloth, and thick paper do not let heat pass through them easily. This teapot is covered with a thick wool **tea cover** to keep the heat in.

This **carryout** coffee is in a special cup that keeps the drink warm. The cup is made of **polystyrene.** Polystyrene is a good insulator.

Using Conductors and Insulators together

The metal plate on the bottom of an **iron** gets very hot. It conducts heat onto the clothes. The plastic handle insulates the person's hand from the heat.

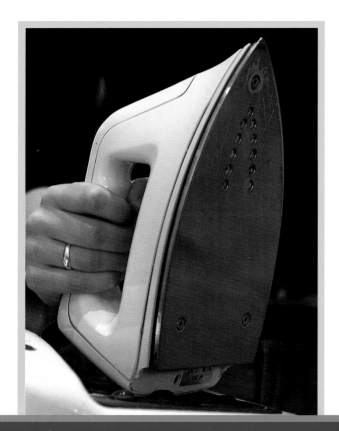

This person is taking a hot dish from an oven. She uses oven gloves to insulate her hands. They do not get burnt.

Glossary

carryout food and drink that you buy in a restaurant to eat and drink in another place

circuit path that allows electricity to flow in a circle

container object used to hold something

copper kind of metal

electric shock violent jolt that happens when electricity flows through a person. A powerful electric shock can kill you.

engine machine that makes something move

fleecy warm, light, and fluffy

gold kind of metal

iron small, heavy machine that uses heat to make clothes smooth

motor engine that uses electricity

polystyrene kind of plastic that is light filled with air

seal to close up

socket hole that an electric plug fits into. The socket joins the plug to electrical wires in the wall.

tea cover cover used to keep a teapot warm

More Books to Read

Burton, Margie, Cathy French, and Tamy Jones. *Heat.* Pelham, N.Y.: Benchmark Edcation Co., 1998.

Riley, Peter D. *Electricity.* Danbury, Conn.: Scholastic Library Publishing, 2000.

Tocci, Salvatore. *Experiments in Electricity.* Danbury, Conn.:Scholastic Library Publishing, 2001.

Index

air 22–23

circuits 12–13

clothes 24–25

conductors 4–5, 19

copper 17, 19

electricity 8–9

engines 11

gold 16

heat 18–19

insulators 6–7, 20–21, 26–27

irons 28

metals 16–17

oven gloves 29

polystyrene 27

safety 9, 14–15

water 14–15

wires 5, 10–11

wool 26